Copyright 2020 - by Beth Costanzo

Machu Picchu which means 'Old Mountain' is a mystical Inca site in the mountains of Peru which is often referred to as the 'Lost City of the Incas.' It is considered one of the Seven Wonders of the World. Machu Picchu is in the Cusco region of Peru, **7950 feet** above the Sacred Valley. The Urubamba River flows past it creating a canyon with a tropical mountain climate.

There are various stories about its origin. Some people suggest that the citadel was once a summer retreat for Kings, while others believe it was inhabited by *Aliens*.

Archaeologists believe that the site was built in approximately **1400 AD** by King Pachacuti. Machu Picchu was re-discovered by explorer *Hiram Bingham* in **1911**.

Machu Picchu is a city comprised of more than **200 buildings**, temples, houses, pathways, fountains and altars all cut from grey granite. There is no evidence of fortified walls, which means that it was not a fortress. Many of the stone blocks weigh more than **50 tons**, and all are cut and fitted together in such a precise manner that it raises as to how they created such a monumental place.

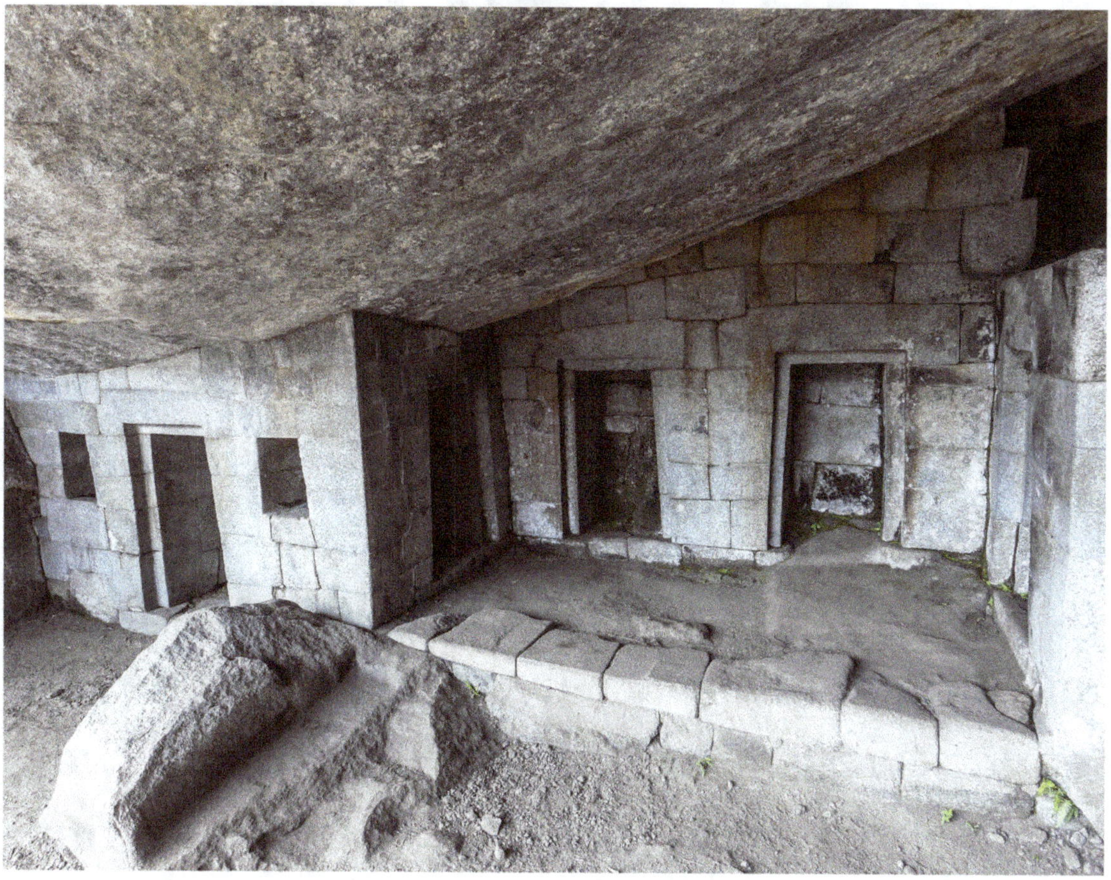

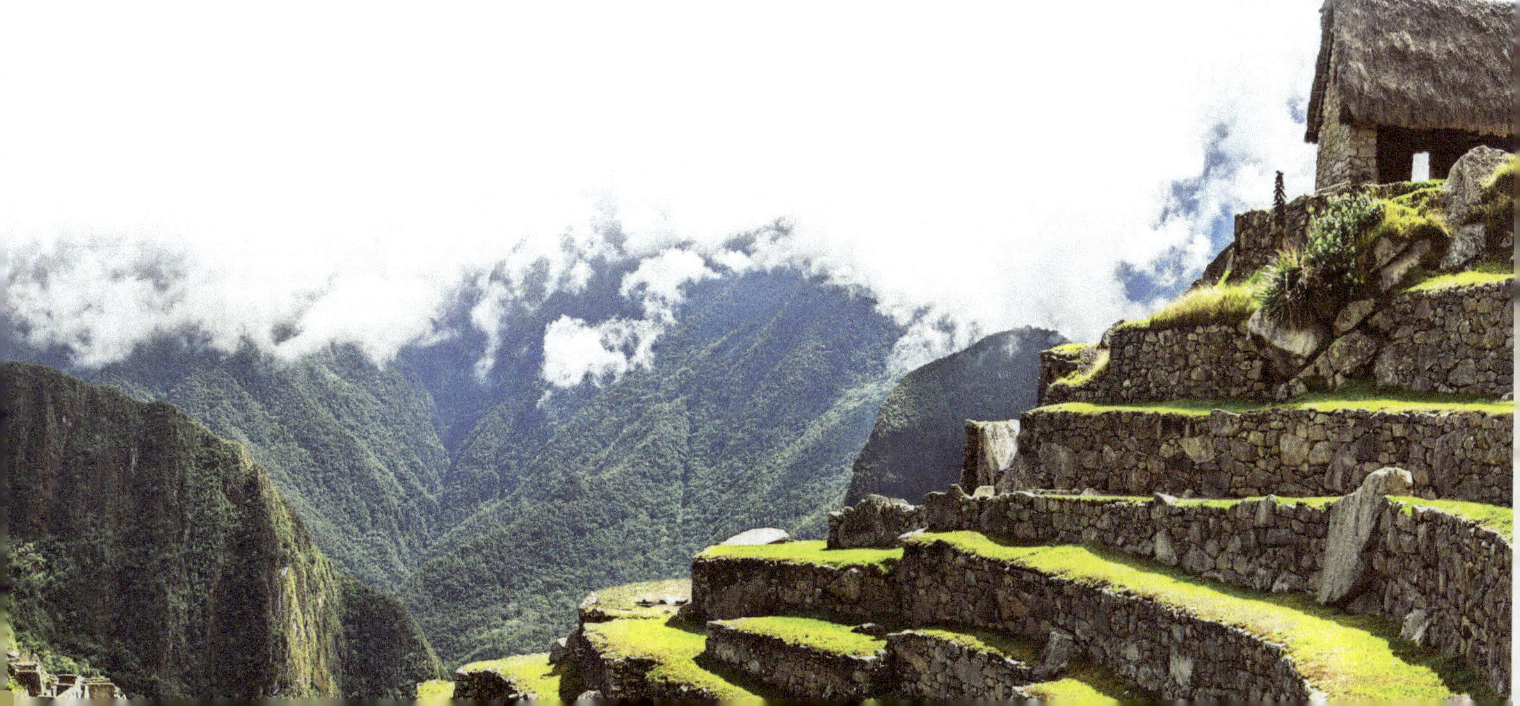

Viracocha

Viracocha was the supreme god of the *Incas*. He was considered the creator god and was the father of all other Inca gods. It was he who formed the earth, heavens, sun, moon and all living beings. When he finished his work he was believed to have travelled far and wide teaching humanity and bringing the civilized arts before he headed west across the Pacific. He was never to be seen again, but promising one day to return. In his absence lesser deities were assigned the duty of looking after the interests of the human race, but Viracocha was always watching the progress of his children.

Viracocha

Pachacutec Creates Machu Picchu

To commemorate his conquest of the *Vilcabamba Valley*, Pachacutec ordered his third royal estate to be built on a high ridge overlooking what is now called the *Urubamba River*. The Incas apparently called the new site Picchu, meaning "peak." From the start, it was planned as a luxurious private estate. The entire complex would display some of the finest examples of Inca engineering and art.

Pachacutec

The complex of what is now known as the *ruins of Machu Picchu* was carefully planned and designed long before the first granite block was ever cut and moved into place. The location had to be both sacred and spectacular. The site that *Pachacuti* selected was set high atop a ridge with an almost God-like view over the entire area. It was essential that the site also contain a source of clean water, a substance sacred in itself-that could be used for drinking, bathing, and for ritual purposes. Picchu possessed just such a crucial characteristic. On the large peak now known as *Machu Picchu*, high above the proposed citadel, Inca engineers located a natural spring. They then designed a gravity-fed water system that would eventually carry water down from the peak to the ridge top site where it would ultimately pass through sixteen descending ritual fountains.

One of the sixteen ritual fountains at Machu Picchu, Peru.

Machu Picchu

How Did They Build This?

There is little information about how or who build Machu Picchu, or how the stones were brought to the mountains. Also, the Inca Empire did not know the wheel, which makes us wonder how they moved the rocks.

The construction has no cement. The stones were cut in polygonal form. The precision of its forms is so exact that some engineers think they were molded by the use of heat, but that does not make sense because that kind of technology was not available.

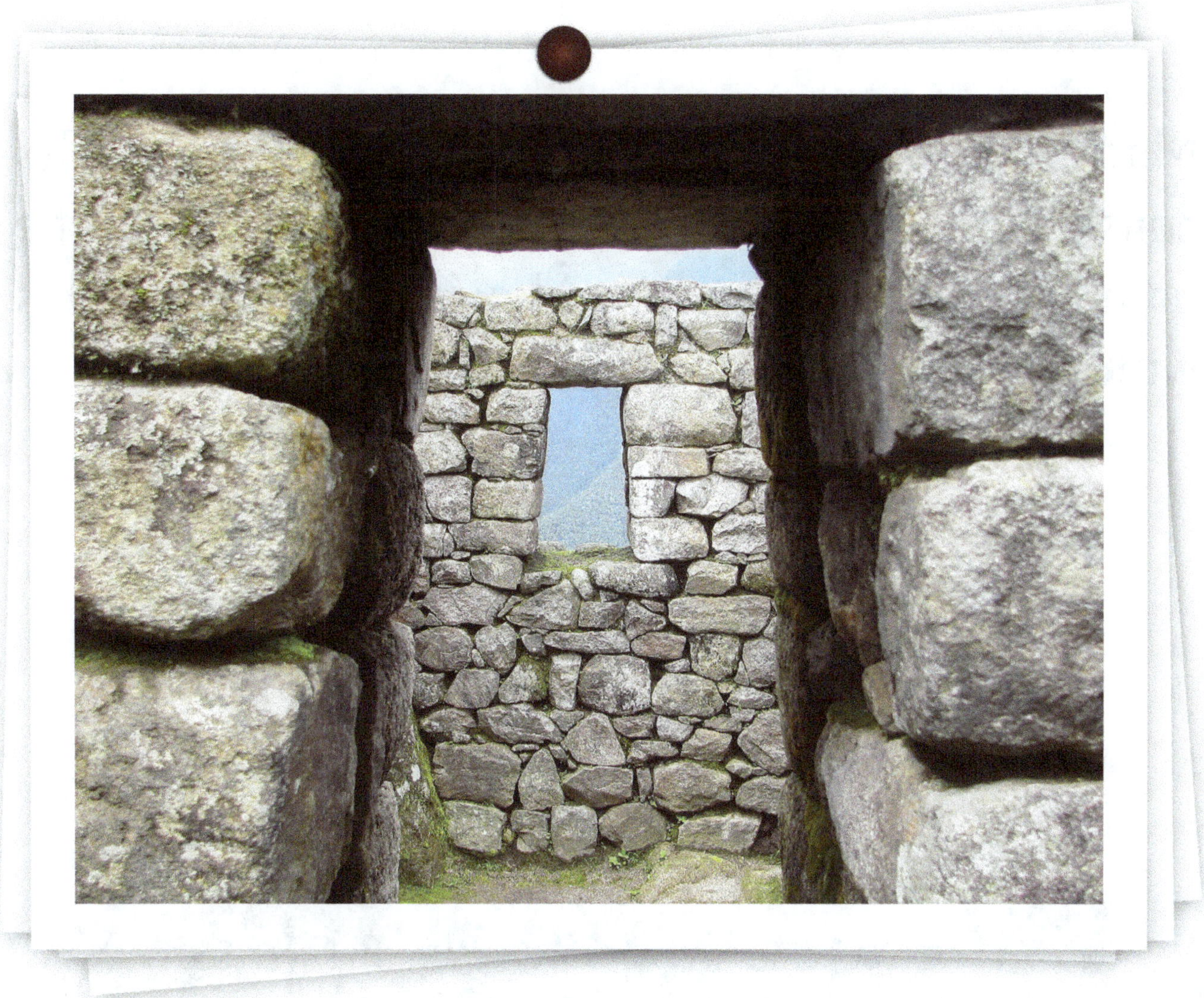

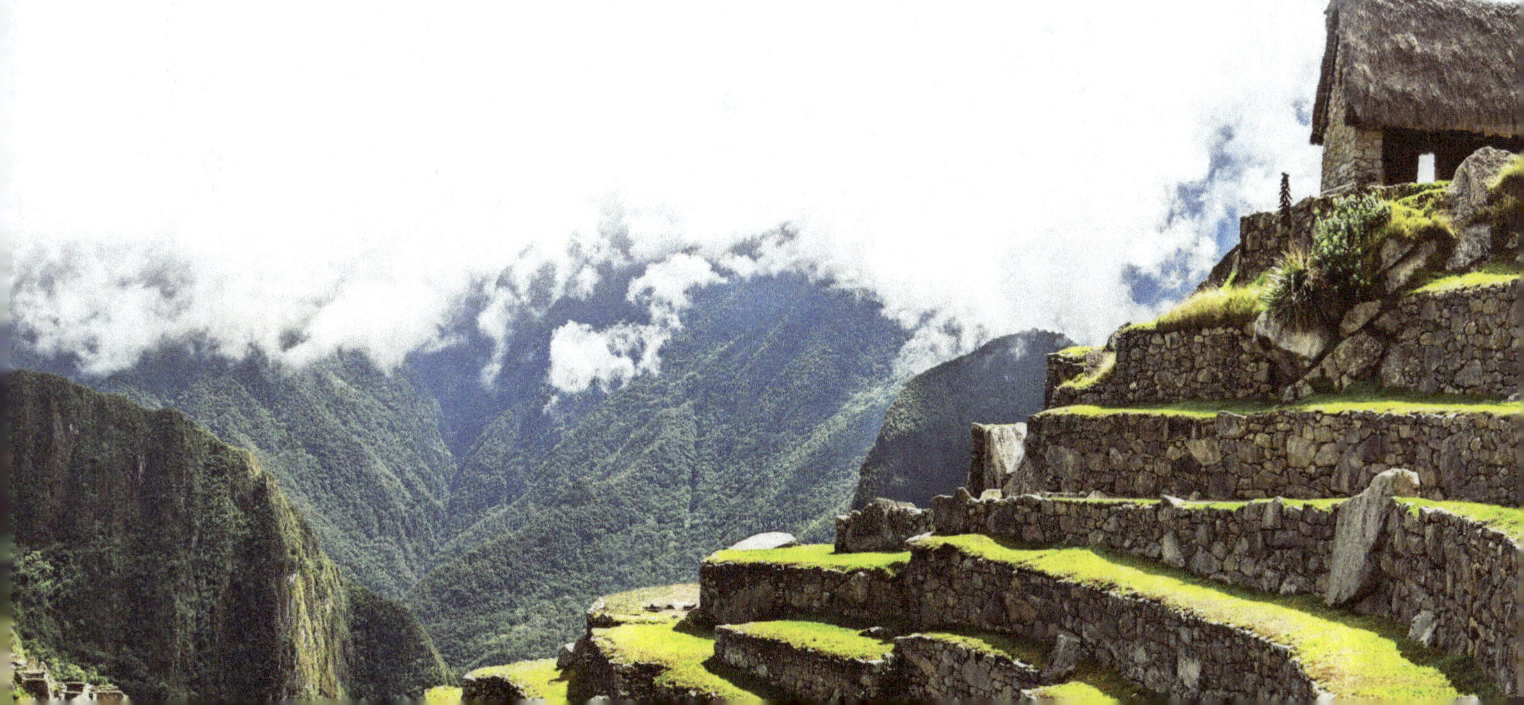

Machu Picchu is a very unique place. Its construction, location and architecture all baffle archaeologists on how and why they built this without modern technology.

Only a few people have permission to enter to this magical and beautiful sanctuary to perform the rituals and ceremonials related to their gods and their principal festivities.

Intihuatana stone as an astronomic clock or calendar by the Incas in Machu Picchu.

One of the functions that archaeologists suggest of this spot is that of astronomical observations. A specific stone at the highest part of the site, the *Intihuatana stone* was used to indicate with accuracy the two equinoxes as well as other celestial events. Local Shamanic legends refer to this stone as a gateway to the spirit world. The person who touches the stone with his forehead would open a vision to the spirit world.

Intihuatana stone

New excavations are currently taking place and recently French mechanic *David Crespi* thinks he discovered a secret entrance that leads to an underground room in the center of the city.

A French Archaeologist named *Thierry Jamin* and team not only confirmed what David suspected, but with the help of instruments verified that many rooms exist below the city and behind the sealed entrance, as well as gold and other precious metals.

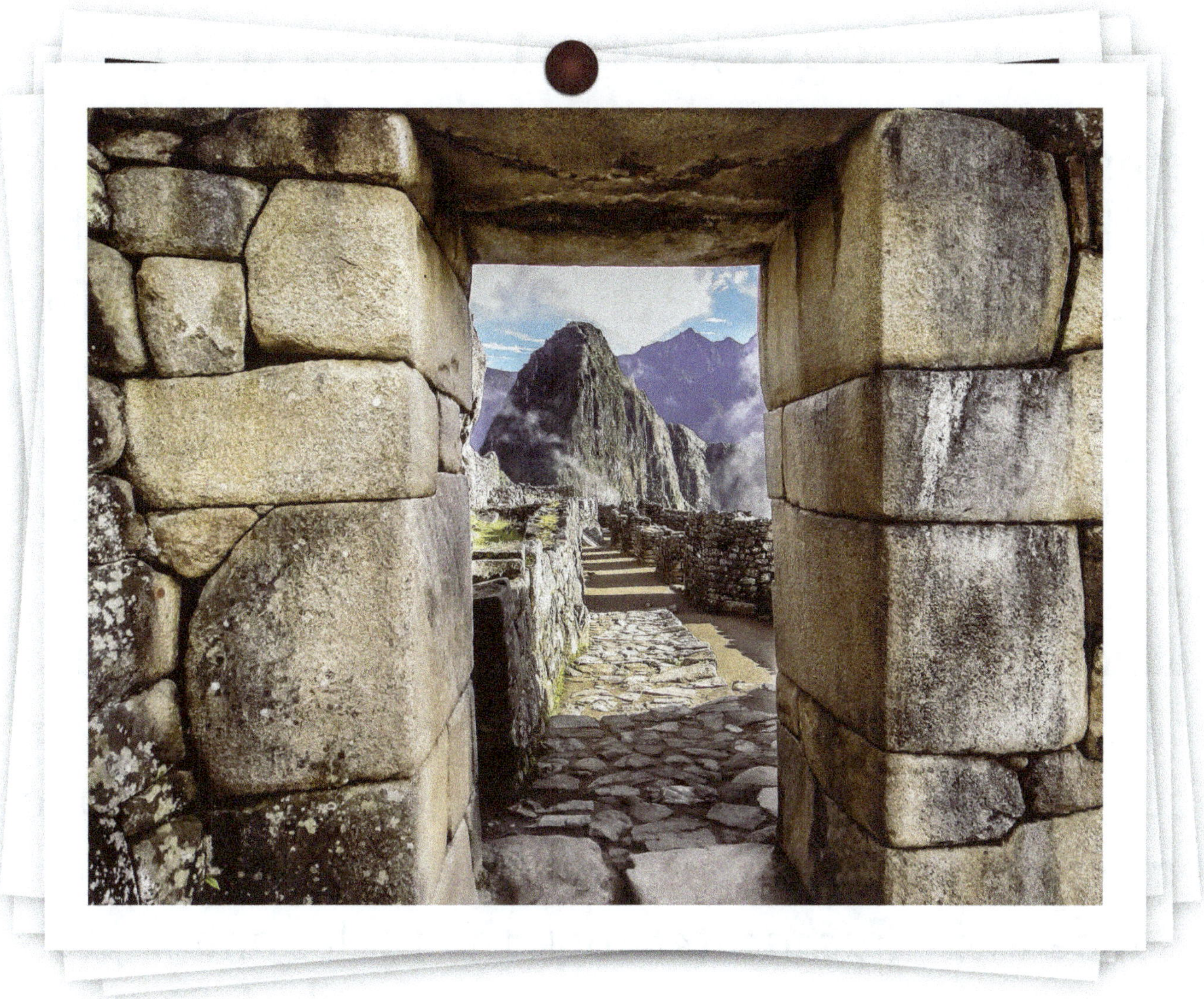

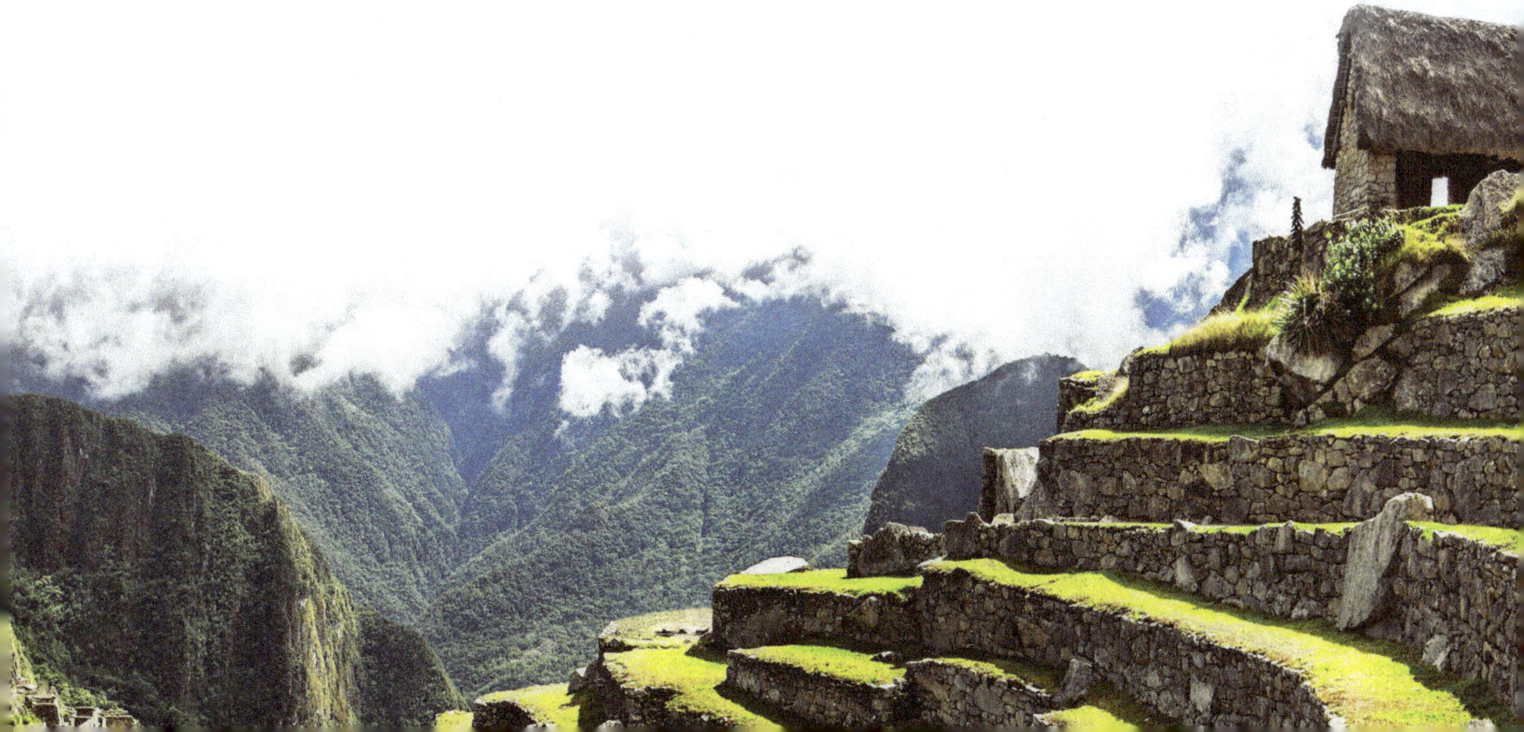

The Legend of Pachacutec

Before Pachacutec became King, he went once to visit his father *Viracocha*. He reached a spring called *Susurpuquiu* and saw a crystal tablet fall into it. The tablet showed a figure of an Indian. He was dressed with a headdress of the Inca's. Three shining rays like the sun sprang from the top of his head. Snakes were coiled around his arms at the shoulder joints. Pachacutec was so afraid he ran. But he heard a voice say, "Come here, my child. Have no fear. I am your father the sun. I know you will honor me and remember me." After saying this, the vision disappeared. *Pachacutec* took the tablet and kept it. After this it served him as a mirror in which he could see anything he wanted. Later he had a statue made of the Sun, which was none other than the image he had seen in the crystal tablet. He later built a temple of the Sun called *Goricancha*.

Peruvian Mummy, Pachacutec

Stone Warriors

The legend of the Pururaucas soldiers or stone soldiers is an Inca legend that mystifies the victory of the Inca army over the Chanca army in 1438.

The Andean legend speaks of a massive battle where the Incas saw themselves outnumbered against a terrifying enemy, but invoked their greatest deity, asking for help.

The god Viracocha responded to their call by turning rocks into soldiers, helping the Inca defend their city causing the enemy to retreat in fear.

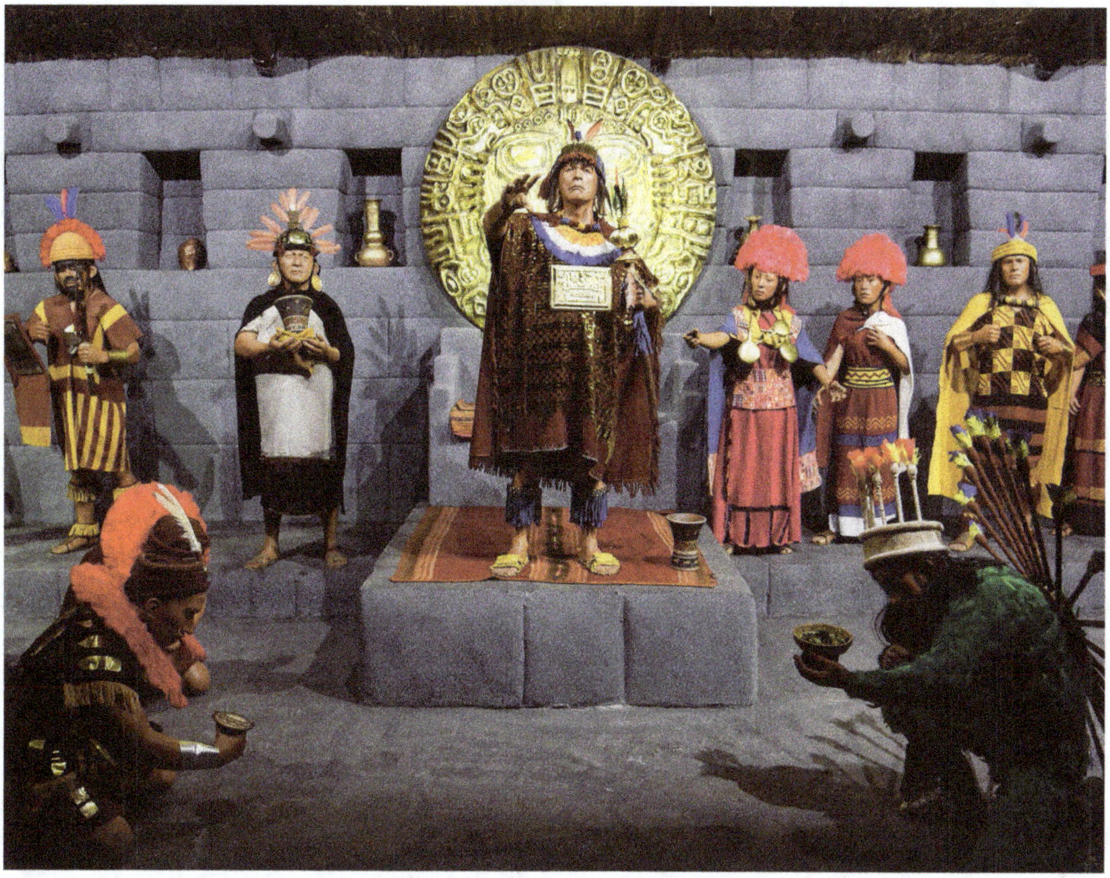

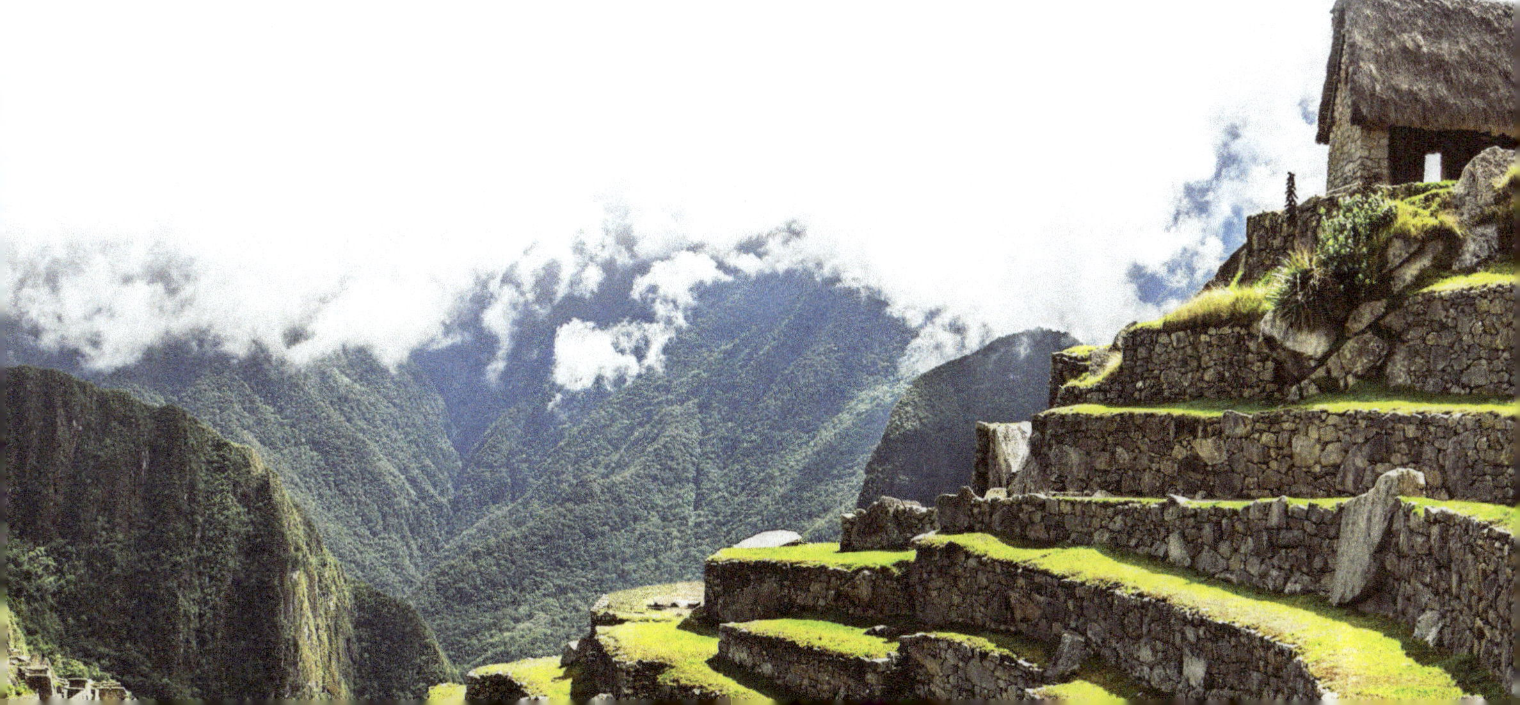

Who built Macchu Picchu and why? How did they manage to move and place such enormous blocks? And most importantly, why was it abandoned? Was this stone city a summer retreat for royalty? Was it built by a technologically advanced human race? Or was it an inter-galactic holiday destination built by *extraterrestrials*?

There is plenty of room for speculation, but when you're standing at the top of Machu Picchu it's difficult to differentiate between fact and fiction. Make up your own mind.

Peruvian People

Macchu Picchu